Pet Care

Poodles

Kelley MacAulay & Bobbie Kalman
Photographs by Marc Crabtree

Crabtree Publishing Company
www.crabtreebooks.com

Poodles

A Bobbie Kalman Book

Dedicated by Marc Crabtree
This book is dedicated to our little Danish friends, Laerke and Line Jakobsen.

Editor-in-Chief
Bobbie Kalman

Writing team
Kelley MacAulay
Bobbie Kalman

Substantive editor
Kathryn Smithyman

Editors
Molly Aloian
Michael Hodge
Rebecca Sjonger

Design
Margaret Amy Salter

Production coordinator
Heather Fitzpatrick

Photo research
Crystal Foxton

Consultant
Dr. Michael A. Dutton, DVM, DABVP, Weare Animal Hospital,
www.weareanimalhospital.com

Special thanks to
Katherine Kantor, Alexander Makubuya, Lakme Mehta-Jones,
Owen Mehta-Jones, Shilpa Mehta-Jones, Samara Parent,
Bailee Setikas, Shelbi Setikas, Sheri Setikas, Katrina Sikkens,
Bonnie Dwyer and Buffy, Sophie, Jorja, and Rocky,
Annie Adams Fox and Michanda Adoreannies Magic

Photographs
All photos by Marc Crabtree except:
Annie Adams Fox of Adoreannies Toy Poodles. (Magic swimming): page 26
iStockphoto.com: Scott Morgan: page 27
© ShutterStock.com/Racheal Grazias: page 6
Comstock: page 19 (meat, egg, and milk)
Ingram Photo Objects: page 19 (chocolate)

Illustrations
Margaret Amy Salter: page 19

Library and Archives Canada Cataloguing in Publication

MacAulay, Kelley
    Poodles / Kelley MacAulay & Bobbie Kalman.

(Pet care)
Includes index.
ISBN-13: 978-0-7787-1763-8 (bound)
ISBN-10: 0-7787-1763-1 (bound)
ISBN-13: 978-0-7787-1795-9 (pbk.)
ISBN-10: 0-7787-1795-X (pbk.)
    1. Poodles--Juvenile literature. I. Kalman, Bobbie, date.
II. Title. III. Series: Pet care

SF429.P85M33 2006   j636.72'8   C2006-904118-0

Library of Congress Cataloging-in-Publication Data

MacAulay, Kelley.
    Poodles / Kelley MacAulay & Bobbie Kalman ; photographs by Marc
Crabtree.
        p. cm. -- (Pet care)
Includes index.
ISBN-13: 978-0-7787-1763-8 (rlb)
ISBN-10: 0-7787-1763-1 (rlb)
ISBN-13: 978-0-7787-1795-9 (pb)
ISBN-10: 0-7787-1795-X (pb)
    1. Poodles--Juvenile literature. I. Kalman, Bobbie. II. Title. III. Series.

SF429.P85M23 2006
636.72'8--dc22
    2006018065

Crabtree Publishing Company

www.crabtreebooks.com   1-800-387-7650

Published in Canada
Crabtree Publishing
616 Welland Ave.
St. Catharines, ON
L2M 5V6

Published in the United States
Crabtree Publishing
PMB16A
350 Fifth Ave., Suite 3308
New York, NY 10118

Published in the United Kingdom
Crabtree Publishing
White Cross Mills
High Town, Lancaster
LA1 4XS

Published in Australia
Crabtree Publishing
386 Mt. Alexander Rd.
Ascot Vale (Melbourne)
VIC 3032

Contents

What are poodles?

Poodles are a **breed**, or type, of dog. Dogs are **mammals**. Mammals are animals that have **backbones**. A backbone is a row of bones in the middle of an animal's back. Mammals have hair or fur on their bodies. A baby mammal drinks milk from its mother's body.

A poodle's body

eye

ear

tail

snout

coat

paw

nail

Pretty poodles

There are three sizes of poodles—**standard**, **miniature**, and **toy**. Standard poodles are large poodles. They usually grow to be more than fifteen inches (38 cm) tall. Miniature poodles are medium-sized poodles. They are usually between ten and fifteen inches (25-38 cm) tall. Toy poodles are small poodles. Toy poodles grow to be less than ten inches (25 cm) tall. This book is about toy poodles.

black toy poodle

brown toy poodle

cream toy poodle

Toy poodles have curly coats. Their coats can be many colors, including silver, apricot, brown, black, cream, or even blue!

Poodle history

Some people believe that poodles are from Germany. Other people believe that poodles are from France. Standard poodles were the first kind of poodle. They are good swimmers. Standard poodles often worked with hunters. After hunters shot birds above lakes, the poodles went into the water to **retrieve**, or bring in, the birds.

*Poodle owners first **clipped**, or cut, the coats of standard poodles to make it easier for the dogs to swim. Before the coats were clipped, a poodle's legs got caught in its long coat.*

Pet poodles

Toy and miniature poodles have been popular pets for hundreds of years. In the 1700s, toy poodles were common pet dogs with the **royal** families of many countries. Many other wealthy people also had toy poodles as pets. Hunters still worked with standard poodles, however. Over time, all types of poodles became popular pets.

The right pet for you?

Poodles make great pets. They do not **shed**, or lose their fur, as much as some other dog breeds do. Since poodles do not shed very much, people who are **allergic** to dog fur may be able to own poodles without feeling sick. Toy poodles are usually nervous dogs, however. They like their homes to be calm. Are there small children living in your home? If so, a toy poodle may not be the right dog for you.

*Toy poodles are intelligent, so they are easy to **train**. This poodle has been trained to "sit" when it is told.*

Are you ready?

Before you add a toy poodle to your family, gather your family together and answer the questions below.

 Who will feed your toy poodle every day?

 Toy poodles have a lot of energy. Are you willing to walk your poodle every day?

 It can cost a lot of money every year to feed a toy poodle, to pay for its health care, and to have it **groomed**, or brushed and cleaned. Is your family willing to pay for all your poodle's needs?

 Will you spend time every day training your toy poodle?

 Toy poodles need a lot of attention. Will you give your toy poodle the attention it needs?

 Grooming a toy poodle can take a lot of time. Are you willing to spend time grooming your pet every day?

Toy poodles can live for up to fifteen years! Will you care for your poodle for its entire life?

Picking your poodle

Before your family buys a toy poodle, ask your friends and **veterinarian** if they know of any poodles that people are giving away. An **animal shelter** in your area may have a toy poodle. You can also buy a poodle from a pet store or a **breeder**. Make sure you get your poodle from people that take good care of animals!

Poodle papers

If you get your poodle from a breeder, the breeder will be able to give you papers that prove your pet is **purebred**. A purebred dog has parents and grandparents that are the same breed. If you want proof that your pet is purebred, you should get the dog from a breeder.

Choose carefully

When picking your poodle, study its behavior and body to make sure it is healthy. A healthy poodle has:

- an energetic, playful personality

- clean ears

- clean, white teeth

- clear, bright eyes

- a damp nose

- no sores on its skin

- a shiny coat with no bald patches

Choosing a toy poodle can be difficult! Take time to get to know a poodle before choosing it as your pet.

Poodle puppies

Before you choose a toy poodle, you must decide if you want an adult dog or a **puppy**. A puppy is a baby dog. Poodle puppies are small and playful. Caring for puppies is not easy, however. Puppies need people around them all the time. Will someone in your family be home all day with the puppy? If not, you may want to get an adult dog. They are cute and playful, too!

Your puppy may be nervous and lonely when it first comes to your home. It may miss its mother. Your puppy will sleep better if you put a ticking clock next to its bed.

Happy housebreaking

If you get a puppy, you will have to train it to go to the bathroom outdoors. This training is called **housebreaking**. Begin housebreaking your puppy as soon as you bring it home. To housebreak your puppy, put it on its leash and take it outdoors about ten minutes after it eats or drinks. Take your pet to the same spot each time. Your puppy will learn to go to the bathroom in that spot. Give your puppy a lot of praise each time it goes to the bathroom outdoors. Soon your puppy will learn to get your attention when it needs to go out.

If you get an older toy poodle, it may already be housebroken. If your pet is not housebroken, lay some newspapers around your house. The papers will protect your floors if your pet has an accident.

13

Preparing for your poodle

You will need many supplies to care for your toy poodle properly. Make sure you have everything shown on these pages before bringing your pet home.

Your toy poodle will need a bowl for water and a bowl for food.

*Your pet should always wear a **collar** and a **tag** that has your phone number on it. Your vet can also use a needle to place a **microchip** with your address in it under your dog's skin. If your pet gets lost, people can use the tag or microchip to return your pet to you.*

collar

tag

Before taking your toy poodle outdoors, attach a leash to its collar to keep your pet from running away.

Your toy poodle should always have some toys.

Get some dog **nail clippers** to keep your toy poodle's nails trimmed.

bristle brush

You will need a **bristle brush** and a **steel comb** to groom your poodle's coat. Make sure the comb has teeth that are about one inch (2.5 cm) long.

steel comb

Your toy poodle will need its own toothbrush and toothpaste made just for dogs.

Buy some treats for your pet. Use the treats as rewards when you train your dog.

Get your toy poodle a large **crate** to use as a **den**, or a safe space.

Make sure your toy poodle has a comfortable bed in which to rest.

The perfect home

Toy poodles can live comfortably in large, spacious homes or in small homes such as apartments. Poodles have a lot of energy, however. You will have to take your toy poodle for a walk every day.

Gentle treatment

Toy poodles are happiest living in homes where there are no small children. Toy poodles are small dogs, and they get nervous easily. Even small children seem big to toy poodles! Young children may chase toy poodles or treat them harshly. When toy poodles feel scared, they may bite to protect themselves. Older children are more likely to treat toy poodles gently.

Show your friends how to treat your poodle.
Make sure everyone is gentle with your pet.

Healthy meals

Toy poodles are often fussy eaters. Do not let your toy poodle decide what it eats. Feed your poodle only healthy foods. Adult dogs need two meals a day. Ask your veterinarian, or "vet," which kind of dog food is healthiest for your pet. Also ask your vet how much food your toy poodle needs at each meal.

Many meals

In order to grow up healthy, puppies need to eat a lot of food. They need four meals every day until they are three months old. When your puppy is three months old, begin feeding it three times a day. When your poodle puppy is six months old, it can begin eating twice a day.

Feed your poodle at the same time every day.

Plenty of water

Your toy poodle should always have a bowl of fresh water to drink. It does not need to drink anything but water. Wash your pet's food and water dishes every day.

Not on the menu

Certain foods are unhealthy for your toy poodle to eat. Some foods that are unsafe for your pet are listed below.

 Never let your toy poodle chew on bones. Your pet could choke on them.

 Dairy foods such as milk can make your pet sick.

 Do not feed **raw** eggs or raw meat to your toy poodle. Raw foods are uncooked.

 Even small amounts of chocolate can make your poodle very sick.

Good-looking poodles

Toy poodles need a lot of grooming. They usually do not like to be groomed, however. Be gentle as you groom your pet. Talk to your dog softly to make grooming more enjoyable for it. An adult should help you groom your poodle.

Coat care

A toy poodle's coat never stops growing. It must be clipped by a **dog groomer**. If your poodle's coat is clipped short, it will be easier for you to brush. Every day, use a steel comb to brush the top of your toy poodle's head gently. Then use a bristle brush to groom the rest of its coat, including the ears. If your poodle's coat is **matted**, or tangled, use the steel comb to untangle the fur. Be careful not to pull hard.

Always brush your toy poodle before and after bathing it. Bathe your poodle about once a month using dog shampoo.

Neat nails

An adult should trim your toy poodle's nails every few weeks using nail clippers made for dogs. Only a small section at the end of each nail needs trimming. If too much of the nail is cut off, the nail will bleed. If the nail bleeds, use **styptic powder** to stop the bleeding. If your poodle's nail continues to bleed after using the styptic powder, take it to the vet right away.

When you brush your poodle, look into its ears. Sometimes a poodle's fur grows down into its ears. Gently pull out the fur. If you see sores or a lot of wax inside the ears, take your pet to the vet.

Terrific training

Spend fifteen to twenty minutes every day teaching your toy poodle how to behave. Toy poodles are intelligent dogs. They usually learn things easily. Be gentle with your poodle while you train it. Never hit your pet or yell at it. This behavior will make your poodle afraid of you. If you are kind to your poodle, it will trust you more and learn faster!

After each training session, spend time playing with your poodle. Your poodle will soon look forward to its training sessions.

Lie down

You can teach your toy poodle to "lie down." Use treats to help your pet learn. Show your poodle a treat. Then tell your poodle to "lie down." Use your hand to guide your pet's bottom to the ground. Move the treat down toward the ground and say "lie down." If your poodle does not lie down, gently lift its front legs and extend them out until it is lying down. Then give your poodle the treat and praise it.

Poodle play

Your toy poodle needs toys. If your poodle does not have toys, it will chew on your belongings, which could harm your dog. Five toys are enough to keep your poodle busy. If you have more toys for the poodle, put them away. Change your poodle's toys every month. Changing the toys will help keep your poodle interested in them.

Toy poodles often like toys that make squeaky sounds!

Safe toys

Use these tips to make sure your poodle's toys are safe, as well as fun.

- Do not give your poodle hard plastic toys or tennis balls. These toys can break into pieces when your pet chews on them. Your toy poodle may choke on the pieces.

- If your poodle has soft toys, make sure the toys do not have hard parts that could come off. Soft toys should be filled with soft material, not beads.

- Dogs like to chase balls. Buy balls that are large enough that your poodle will not choke on them.

Find the toy!

Play with your poodle every day. Try playing a game with your poodle by hiding a toy and helping your pet find it. First, show your poodle the toy. Let the dog sniff the toy. Then have a friend gently hold your pet while you hide the toy somewhere close by. Come back to your pet and tell it to "find the toy!" Help your poodle find the toy by using an excited tone of voice when the poodle is close to the hiding spot.

When your poodle finds the toy, reward it with a lot of praise!

Water dogs

Toy poodles enjoy being in water. They are good swimmers. Swimming is a good way for your poodle to stay fit. If you keep your toy poodle's coat short, your pet will be able to swim more easily. Gently dry inside your poodle's ears with a towel after it swims.

This toy poodle is swimming in a pool.

Time to learn

Learning to swim may be scary for your toy poodle. Do not force your poodle into water. Take your pet to a beach and allow it to follow you into the water. Swim around and let your poodle follow you. When your pet is comfortable in water, it will be able to swim by itself.

Safety rules

Make sure that your poodle is safe around water. The rules below will help you keep your pet safe.

- Never let your poodle swim in water with strong **currents**. Currents are rushing water that could pull your pet under water.

- Never let your poodle swim in unclean water.

- Do not allow your poodle to swim in very cold water.

- Never leave your poodle alone while it swims. Watch your pet carefully whenever it is in water.

- Do not let your poodle swim for long periods of time. Your poodle may not know when it is too tired to keep swimming.

- If your poodle is swimming in a pool, make sure it can get out easily. Give your pet a bath after it swims in a pool.

Safety tips

Your toy poodle may be small and soft, but it is definitely not a toy! You have to respect your poodle's **territory**, or personal space. For example, if you bother your pet while it is eating or sleeping in its crate, it may try to protect its territory. Toy poodles often bite to protect their space. Teach your poodle to share its space.

Toy poodles do not like to be teased. Teasing can make your pet angry. Instead, give your poodle praise when it behaves well!

Watch for signs

You may be able to tell when your poodle is getting **aggressive**, or angry. Your pet may growl or show its teeth. If your poodle behaves this way, do not look the poodle in the eyes. Stand still and hold your arms at your sides. Say "good dog" in a soothing voice to try to calm down your pet. When the dog calms down, tell an adult how the dog behaved.

Always be gentle with your pet, so that it knows you will never hurt it.

Healthy poodles

As soon as you get your toy poodle, take it to a vet. The vet will give your dog a checkup and make sure it is healthy. The vet may also give your poodle **vaccinations** with needles to keep it from getting sick. Take your poodle to see the vet at least once every year for a checkup.

Your vet can answer all your questions about toy poodles.

No puppies!

You should have your toy poodle **neutered**. A neutered dog cannot make puppies. If you let your poodle have puppies, you will have to work hard to find good homes for all the puppies.

Signs of sickness

Poodles usually live long lives, but they still get sick. Take your poodle to a vet if you notice any of the warning signs below.

 Toy poodles can develop sore hips. If your poodle is having trouble walking, it may have sore hips.

 Many poodles have problems with their gums. You can help prevent these problems by brushing your poodle's teeth. If your pet's gums are bleeding, take it to a vet.

 Take your poodle to the vet right away if it is vomiting, fainting, or limping.

Your pet may be sick if it loses large clumps of fur.

Your poodle's ears and eyes should be clean, and you should not feel any lumps on its body.

 A sick poodle may drink more water than usual. It may also stop eating.

If your poodle is sleeping a lot and is not playful, take it to the vet.

A good friend

Toy poodles are loyal and loving pets. With proper care, your toy poodle will be your good friend for many years!

Words to know

Note: Boldfaced words that
are defined in the book may
not appear on this page.

allergic Describing someone who
has a physical reaction to something

animal shelter A place that cares
for animals that do not have owners

breeder A person who brings
dogs together so the dogs
can make puppies

dairy food Food made with milk
and milk products

dog groomer A person who cleans
and brushes dogs for a living

microchip A small device that
can be placed under an animal's
skin and that holds information

royal Describing a king or queen
or a member of the king's or
queen's family

styptic powder A powder used
to stop bleeding

train To teach a dog how to
behave properly

vaccination A way of protecting
a body against diseases

veterinarian A doctor who
treats animals

Index

Printed in the U.S.A.